Project Management

B. Vincent

Published by RWG Publishing, 2021.

While every precaution has been taken in the preparation of this book, the publisher assumes no responsibility for errors or omissions, or for damages resulting from the use of the information contained herein.

PROJECT MANAGEMENT

First edition. June 8, 2021.

Copyright © 2021 B. Vincent.

Written by B. Vincent.

Also by B. Vincent

Affiliate Marketing
Affiliate Marketing

Standalone
Affiliate Recruiting
Business Layoffs & Firings
Business and Entrepreneur Guide
Business Remote Workforce
Career Transition
Project Management

ESPLR Project Management

Someone once said, project management is like juggling three balls, time, cost, and quality. And it's true, project management requires you to balance a lot of difficult variables and the stakes are high. In many cases, the very life of a business itself may depend on the ability of its project managers to keep operations running smoothly and efficiently. Project management can be described as the art of initiating, planning, executing, controlling, and closing the work of a team to achieve specific goals and meet specific success criteria, by a specified time. But how can you ensure that you or the project managers in your organization are operating at peak performance? In this course, we're going to help you do exactly that.

Only 58% of organizations fully understand the value of project management.

Project failures cost the US economy, approximately 150 billion, each year. Organizations that invest in proven project management practices waste 28 times less resources, because more of their strategic initiatives are successfully completed.

Our course is going to consist of a series of critical discussion points. These are designed to cover this broad topic as thoroughly as possible, to encourage growth in these vital areas, and to facilitate a real and fruitful discussion with your organization, about how you can each improve on these essential characteristics both at work and in your personal lives in general. Some of these will be pretty lengthy and some will be relatively straightforward and brief. At the very end of this roadmap comes the most important final step. Discussion time do not skip this. This is the most important part of this training.

When you finish this course, you will need to spend about an hour at least going over questions that we supply at the end as a group, whoever's the head honcho on the group should designate a facilitator whose responsibility it is, that each question is covered, and everyone, time permitting, is able to have their say. Make sure all contributions are valued, all suggestions considered, and all opinions respected. So, let's move into the first discussion point, about project management.

Have all the project details, make sure that your project is based on a solid foundation, and that you were able to get all the key stakeholders to buy into the success and results of the project. The adage of failing to plan is planning to fail still holds true for project management. Proper planning takes a lot of organization, attention to detail, and close involvement from your team. Understand the interests and expectations of the stakeholders and be aware of how they will determine whether or not the project is successful, the project scope should be properly identified, including the roles and responsibilities of the various project team members. Ensure that the goals of the key elements are clearly defined and closely aligned. Establish measurable and trackable success criteria.

Focus on the final team outcome, in project management, it can be easy to go into analysis paralysis. When several other people are handling and completing a project and taking charge of certain aspects of it, sometimes it can get difficult to stay focused on the final picture. In the end, everyone's work should come together cohesively, ensure that everyone is able to set aside their biases for the successful congruency of the overall picture. It's a lot easier to work together when everyone is focused on the final outcome, and not on the hugging the spotlight for themselves.

Set realistic expectations, be certain that everyone on the team, including the client, understands the limitations of the project. A project can be successfully completed on time and within budget, as long as everyone's expectations are reasonable. Remember that you're not capable of working miracles. This means that if expectations are not reasonable from the beginning, you're only setting yourself up for a world of failure. Don't start your project with failure clearly predestined.

Identify requirements for projects and team members, assemble an effective project team, the project team is defined as a working unit of individual components, having a shared goal, reached through the systematic application of aggregate skills. Make sure that skill sets align with required goals. As a project manager, you'll have to align the skills, talents, and personalities of each team member with the appropriate project needs. Make sure that each individual working on the project is clear about their task and what they're providing upon completion. Remember that if you assign the wrong person to a task, it reduces the chances of success.

Have your team's support, all the technology in the world won't make you an effective project manager, if your team is not behind you. Earn your team's trust by listening to them, especially when it comes to project risks and obstacles, you'll make more informed decisions if you've got a firm handle on your team's abilities.

Identify roles, make sure each team member is clear on what's expected from them, and when. Furthermore, be certain that you also understand your own rule and your delegated authority. This will be dependent upon the kind of organization we're operating under. You should also keep your key stakeholders at their level of influence in mind, the RACI model can help you with this. It's ideal for clarifying roles and responsibilities, especially when there are cross-functional processes, R means who is responsible to do the work. A stand for who is accountable for final decisions and ultimate ownership, C who is consulted before a decision or action is taken, and I, who is informed that the decision or action has been taken.

Beware of role creep, this is similar to scope creep in a project. As a project manager, you'll be under constant pressure. This is due to the fact that there's lots of forces at play for any sizable project especially in the environments where there's no discipline to comply with standardized and repeatable project management processes. We are constantly facing pressures to be more innovative, or more creative. You will even have to face your bosses who will ask you to list all your accomplishments regularly. Despite the constant pressures that you'll encounter, don't forget that your ultimate objective is always to deliver what is in the project plan, let your team do their jobs, and don't force them to take on the workloads that are beyond their skills, especially when time is of the essence.

Communicate well, good communication with your team helps you identify deviations promptly. As a project manager, building your network and understanding company culture and dynamics are very important for the success of any project you handle. Always allow people to come to you, be accessible and listen to what your team members ask or say, keep in mind that the more you know, the more informed you will be when it's time to make a decision. Respect every opinion as if it were your own. Even when you don't agree, make sure that your team members know that you respect and value what they have to say, use more interactive communication. This will allow everyone to acknowledge the receipt of any information and respond with questions for clarification. Plan your project meetings ahead of time. Meetings tend to have a bad reputation for being a huge waste of time. However, if you plan ahead and have a clear agenda, and head before you enter the conference room, you will avoid falling into time-wasting traps. You must communicate any perceived risks, roadblocks, or challenges beforehand, be transparent with the team and let them know nothing will stand in your way.

Set, deliverables, in project management, the term deliverables is conventionally used to refer to the quantifiable goods or services that must be given upon completion of a project. These deliverables may be tangible or intangible in nature. To be an effective project manager, you must always identify these deliverables, ahead of time, especially when you have more variables to take into account.

Furthermore, you should take the time to find out from your team and stakeholders what the deliverables should be, and when they should be given.

Manage expectations with stakeholders. Stakeholders can be any person or group that has a vested stake in the success of a project program or portfolio. It can be individual team members, functional groups, sponsors, vendors, and definitely customers. Expectations of all stakeholders must be carefully identified, communicated, and managed, missing this can lead to misunderstandings, conflict, and even project failure.

In case of a situation or challenge unexpectedly occurring. Be proactive by warning your stakeholders beforehand. The last thing you want to do is surprise them with bad news especially when the project is coming to an end, what their stakeholders know about the possible consequences of the situation, and make sure that you have a plan of action moving forward to address the problem. Keep it simple, and always offer a solution. Specify the actions you'll need from them and make sure they're always up to date on the status of the project.

Keep work organized, keeping your work organized should be your number one priority, manage your time wisely, and use effective project management tools, so you will always be able to track what work is being done in which tasks are already completed. Make sure that you maintain a balance between being productive during the productive hours at work, and allowing employees to have their free time, your team should be able to get the work done on time without being stressed out because you're pressuring them, laying out tasks and targets for employees to meet during each day is a good way to start.

Document everything, be prepared to keep a paper trail so that if something goes wrong, you'll know where to start looking. Here's some tips to keep in mind when documenting the project: keep detailed notes, make notes on each step, including what went right or wrong, who did what, and why they did it. Always provide positive reinforcement and place negatives in a positive light if you need to, work smarter, not harder. Use software to make documentation easier. The more details you have laid out in the writing, the better.

Understand the details, internalize them, everything from stakeholder expectations to final goals, communicate these expectations and details to your team members, particularly when it concerns their responsibilities.

Manage your time wisely, as a project manager, time management skills are crucial because you'll be dealing with an extensive range of tasks that require a quick turnaround time. Getting things done involves keeping your responsibilities organized and increasing your productivity. You can also use project management software to help you track the work of you and your team. If you don't have the time to learn how to use a new tool or software. A simple to-do list can also be a great organizational tool. Prioritize your most critical tasks by placing them at the top of the list and the less important ones at the bottom. Having this visual plan of your daily responsibilities will keep you on track and more aware of time.

Adopt a methodology, every project manager knows that adopting the right methodology is essential to getting the job right. For example, there's the waterfall methodology which is straightforward and linear. The name is appropriate because the waterfall methodology involves a process, we're in the phase of the project's flow downward. The model requires that you move from one phase to another only after a phase has been successfully completed. There's the critical path method where you create a model of the project, which includes all the activities for the work breakdown structure. The duration of each task, any task dependencies, and milestones to larger phases of the project or points in which your deliverables are due. There's the agile method, which is an evolving and collaborative way, to self-organize across teams. The work is adaptive in planning evolutionary and creation, its main goal is early delivery, as always open to changes such change can result in improvements. Then there's Scrum, scrum is a short sprint approach to project management. It's ideal for small teams with 10 members or less, and it's widely used in software development, although it can easily be applied to any industry or business such as retail logistics, event planning, or any project that requires some flexibility.

Keep meetings focused, meetings that go on and on it can get very annoying, especially when people are talking in circles. As a project manager, it's your responsibility to make sure that people don't go off on tangents or give endless speeches. Make the purpose of the meeting clear, you can prevent so many problems by clearly identifying the reason for the get-together at the very start, creating the agenda, and limit it to three main points. This can allow for sufficient time to be spent on important topics and to avoid wasting time.

Meetings can get out of control if there's too many people in the room. For this reason, only include the people who are critical to the meeting. Don't feel like you have to invite everyone but be sure to send out a memo and update everyone else afterward, so they know what's happening. Set the right tone, instead of using the time to convince people of your viewpoint, be open to hearing other's perspectives. Don't be afraid of being wrong. If you have a team member who's prone to rambling, talk with them ahead of time and ask that they keep their comments to a minimum, so that others can be heard.

Define critical milestones, the success of the project depends on the identification of the defining moments throughout the project. These milestones are effective indicators of the team's working cohesively, to complete the project successfully.

Furthermore, critical milestones can be used to manage risks and track progress, identify critical milestones throughout the project. You can provide a life cycle of the project by including the four primary phases initiation, planning, execution, and closure. And make sure you do a comprehensive evaluation at the end of each phase.

Establish measurable and reportable criteria for success. You should always have a way to measure success if you want to know whether or not your project is going as planned. Critical milestones, especially for a project that'll spend a long period of time, will help you to determine if you're keeping on track or straying from the project's objects. At the same time, you should also have both internal checkpoints and client checkpoints. Don't put off asking for feedback until the very end, unless you want to have to risk going back and redoing a whole bunch of work.

Budget wisely, employee sound budget management skills. Most companies, no matter how large or small, tighten their belts and operate within the confines of a finite amount of resources. This can put a lot of pressure on you as the project manager. You have to have a habit of managing financial elements in your control. If we don't approach it regularly and routinely, you'll find the job becomes so huge, it's impossible to do. Always consider the costs of spontaneous attacks or surprises. Think about what the stakeholders really need and want, make sure that everyone is accountable, as well as informed on any changes. Develop key performance indicators which take into account the project's long-term goals. If necessary, revise, revisit and review stay on top of the expenses with filing systems that work for invoices quotas and estimates, getting into the habit of using a budgeting software or even just the spreadsheet can really help.

Understand and use the organizational structure, organizations and project teams may be structured in a wide range of ways. For example, they can be organized in a matrix structure wherein team members work on a project but report to different functional managers. They can also be projectile where team members report to only one project manager. As a project manager, you should understand these structures and how to manage their pros and cons to the best possible advantage. For example, if you're using a matrix structure, you'll need to establish positive relationships with functional managers and communicate clear requirements and expectations from them. Remember that the context within which you operate is a critical factor that you should consider when you're still in the planning process.

Know your limitations, one of the biggest challenges that you'll need to deal with as a project manager, or project constraints. These are project limitations which can quickly put your project success at risk. This is why it's important to know all possible constraints, their influences on each other, and how you can effectively address and resolve them.

Some project limitations can include human element limitations. Remember that humans are not robots and we're computers. Software limitations, not all software will work for every project, nor can all software be adapted immediately to project needs. IT limitations, some managers may be guilty of not including IT personnel and stages of software design or procurement, correct this project management limitation by ensuring software and IT needs are interconnected at all times. Vendor and supplier limitations, the suppliers you utilize can also put limits on your project timelines. Make sure you're working with a reliable vendor or supplier to ensure timely delivery.

Manager scope creep, avoiding scope creep is another crucial factor for project success. Scope creep takes place when changes are made to the scope of a project without any control. It's natural for changes to occur to projects at one point or another. However, if you can't control the changes, you'll have little chance of keeping on top of the work and managing the project effectively. Document the requirements by talking to all the project stakeholders and users to work out exactly what they want from the project. Set up a change control process in which, if someone suggests a change, it's reviewed, approved, or rejected. Create a definite project schedule. This is the result of understanding what your project will deliver, and these two will show all the requirements and how they will be obtained through listing down tasks and activities. Verify the scope with all stakeholders, check that you have properly understood the requirements, take the time to go back to your stakeholders and share their requirement documentation as well as the project schedule with them. Make sure that your project team is happy as well. They need to know about the change control process and how it will affect them, explain that they cannot say yes to changes without going through the process first. If they want to help a stakeholder, the best thing to do is explain the change control process and offer to help with documentary.

Use a project management tool, technology has streamlined the way projects are managed and completed. A project management tool serves many functions from file and document storage, to giving feedback, collaboration, and communication with so many tools to choose from today, choose the one that best suits your organization. Remember that the best project management tool is something that combines collaboration, time management, communication planning, and document sharing into a single ecosystem. Planning or scheduling should be one of the features, collaboration should be another, documentation is another good one so you can avoid missing files with file management features. Evaluation is another feature that your project management tool should have, and it allows you to track and assess productivity and growth through resource management and reporting.

Don't micromanage it, you can't manage everything. Let your team members manage individual goals and hold them accountable for their work. Keep in mind that micromanaging not only kills your productivity time but also lowers team morale. Instead, invest your time in the things that matter most for the project. Believe in your team's ability so they can confidently and effectively do their work. If you find yourself guilty of micromanaging a project, here's some tips that you can try. Reflect on your behavior, you need to understand and be aware of why you micromanage. Most likely, it's because you're afraid it'll reflect badly on you if your team doesn't do something exactly the way you would want it. You might also be worried that you'll look out of touch if you're not immersed in the details, so you overcompensate. In a lot of cases, there can be a disconnect between what leaders intend, and what the team is actually experiencing. Feedback is essential to see how significant the issue is, do an anonymous survey to know what your team really thinks about how you manage them. What you hear may be sobering but this will help you change and move forward. Train and delegate, you can't expect all your employees to do good at their job if you're taking on everything yourself, no matter how important you believe the task is. And because your team members are so used to you not trusting them, they may want to come to you for approval before taking charge of a project. Make sure your team members know you can trust them and have faith in their abilities.

Manage potential risks, risk management is essential for project success. Risks are potential threats that can creep up any time and can jeopardize the progress of your project. To ensure that your project is successful, potential risks should be identified ahead of time so that measures can be taken if they come up. Don't turn the risk management into an unnecessary overhead, instead seek to integrate risk management with other project management processes, understand the critical factors which will determine the success or failure of your project. This will help you prioritize and concentrate on managing the risks that may have considerable effect on the outcome of the project. Describe your risks accurately. In this way, you'll be better able to determine mitigations that are concerned with the probability of risk occurrence and mitigations that involve the risk impact separately. After describing a risk, you should then determine which category the risk falls into whether it's minor, moderate, or critical. Being able to analyze the risk immediately, ultimately results in smarter decisions based around that risk. And assign a team member to oversee and own this risk. If there's a team member who is more skilled or experienced with dealing with the assigned risk. This member should then lead this risk to resolve it.

Ask for feedback, having a project fail isn't necessarily a bad thing, but you should learn from your mistakes and make the right changes moving forward. This is why feedback is so crucial. Encourage all stakeholders and project team members to express their opinions and concerns openly and honestly, this will help you avoid mistakes and make sure that all future projects are successful, asking for this feedback will help you form better relationships with your team members. Feedback promotes personal and professional growth and provides positive criticism enables everyone to see what they can change to improve their focus and results. It helps everyone develop their professional skills at the same time increasing the efficiency of the whole team, whether the feedbacks done in person or through a survey, the person providing the feedback needs to know that they have been understood, and they need to know that their feedback provides some value, and feedback can actually motivate your team to perform better. Everybody likes to feel valued and appreciates being asked to provide feedback that can help formulate decisions and even project direction.

Test deliverables, deliverables must be tested at every critical milestone. And the final product should satisfy the project requirements. Before moving on to the next phase of the project, you need to be sure that the project is coming along as planned. At every milestone, the deliverable must meet or exceed expectations to be considered a success. Testing deliverables involves creating a test plan that describes this test strategy, as well as objectives, schedule estimation and deliverables, and resources required for testing. This test plan will essentially serve as a blueprint to determine whether or not the deliverable is able to meet or exceed the expectations of the stakeholder.

Anticipate project setbacks, hope for the best but plan for the worst, preventing a crisis will keep your project running smoothly, save you a lot of time, and keep you, your team, and your stakeholders confident in progressing with the project. Pay attention to complaints from stakeholders or colleagues and other warning signs that there may be an issue, such as a missed deadline or cost overrun. Just keep in mind that even with a high level of planning and attention to detail your project may still face some challenges.

Track and replan, projects sometimes don't go according to plan. Furthermore, project priorities change during the course of a project. This is why you need to constantly revisit, reshape, and refine your plan to make sure you're adjusting accordingly. Periodic replanting can take place upon completing a milestone or after a feedback session with stakeholders. Part of this includes assessing the status of the project, you can use dashboards in your project site meetings with team members and incoming change requests. When reviewing the project, identify any issues or risks, issues refer to risks identified during project planning which have now turned into reality. Find and address as many issues as possible, because these can be the biggest hindrances in the project schedule. Check work reports for late or unassigned tasks and deal with these properly.

Before making major changes to projects, discuss with the stakeholders for advice and authorization. Ensure that all changes are approved and signed off before you start planning for the project. If workloads or tasks change, make sure that the relevant team members are aware of them.

Be a problem solver, sometimes project managers rush into the doing of a project before analyzing all the dependencies and identifying all the risks, pre-emptive problem solving can help you avoid project nightmares later on. However, if anything goes awry with a project, remember that the best lessons come from mistakes, but they're only valuable lessons if you correctly apply what you've learned. Crisis management skills are crucial when dealing with the unexpected. You should also be flexible and pragmatic, improvise and make quick decisions when necessary.

First, you define the problem, next you dig deeper and start determining what's causing it. This level of analysis is crucial to ensure that the solutions you come up with address the actual causes of the problem instead of the symptoms of the problem. Get creative and develop possible solutions to the problem. Two proven problem-solving techniques you can use for coming up with solutions are brainstorming and mind mapping. Use a simple trade-off analysis to decide which solution to go with. If the solution involves several actions or requires actions from others, create an action plan and consider it as a mini project.

Evaluate, you can learn a lot for your next project by taking note of what worked and what didn't work with your current project, review the project as a whole, and analyze various project components. By doing so, you can note down the successes in a project, what went wrong in the project, and what can be improved for future projects. Here are some things you should ask yourself when evaluating projects. What were the project victories? What were the project disappointments?

What can you say about the project's quality and the product's performance? And how does the planned return on investment compare to the actual ROI?

Learn from failures, no matter what anyone else may tell you, failure is an option. However, it's always preferable to fail fast so that you can recover quickly and learn from it. Don't be afraid of making mistakes because they are the building blocks for your future success. Instead, turn your mistakes into learning opportunities.

Hone your skills with project management training. Keep in mind that effective project management requires a set of technical skills. Many of these skills can be acquired by getting various project management certifications. There's a lot of project management training courses available ranging from beginner to advanced. Project management training can also help fill any skill gaps you might be facing or refresh a few of the methodologies and key project management principles you learned a few years ago.

More importantly, having project management certifications is a signal to your boss and future employers and stakeholders that you perform well and that you're committed to quality service.

And now it's discussion time. The most important part of this training, whoever is the head honcho in the group should designate a facilitator, whose responsibility it is that each of the questions you see on your screen is covered. And then everyone, time permitting, is able to have their say. Make sure all contributions are valued, all suggestions considered, and all opinions respected.

Don't miss out!

Visit the website below and you can sign up to receive emails whenever B. Vincent publishes a new book. There's no charge and no obligation.

https://books2read.com/r/B-A-QWUO-RAKPB

BOOKS 2 READ

Connecting independent readers to independent writers.

Also by B. Vincent

Affiliate Marketing
Affiliate Marketing

Standalone
Affiliate Recruiting
Business Layoffs & Firings
Business and Entrepreneur Guide
Business Remote Workforce
Career Transition
Project Management

About the Publisher

Accepting manuscripts in the most categories. We love to help people get their words available to the world.

Revival Waves of Glory focus is to provide more options to be published. We do traditional paperbacks, hardcovers, audio books and ebooks all over the world. A traditional royalty-based publisher that offers self-publishing options, Revival Waves provides a very author friendly and transparent publishing process, with President Bill Vincent involved in the full process of your book. Send us your manuscript and we will contact you as soon as possible.

Contact: Bill Vincent at rwgpublishing@yahoo.com www.rwgpublishing.com

www.ingramcontent.com/pod-product-compliance
Lightning Source LLC
Chambersburg PA
CBHW060346080526
44583CB00014B/1080